COOKING
THE
AUSTRALIAN
WAY

Lerner Publications Company
A division of Lerner Publishing Group
241 First Avenue North
Minneapolis, MN 55401 U.S.A.

Website address: www.lernerbooks.com

Library of Congress Cataloging-in-Publication Data

Germaine, Elizabeth.
    Cooking the Australian way / Elizabeth Germaine & Ann L.
Burckhardt.—Rev. and expanded.
        p.   cm. — (Easy menu ethnic cookbooks)
    Includes index.
    Summary: An introduction to the cooking of Australia, featuring such
recipes as egg and bacon pie, Anzac biscuits, pumpkin soup, and glazed
kiwi tart. Also includes information on the history, geography, customs
and people of the "land down under."
    ISBN: 0–8225–4101–7 (lib. bdg. : alk. paper)
    1. Cookery, Australian—Juvenile literature. 2. Australia—Social life and
customs—Juvenile literature. [1. Cookery, Australian. 2. Australia—Social
life and customs.] I. Burckhardt, Ann, 1933– II. Title. III. Series.
TX725.A9 G47 2004
641.5994—dc21   2002153396

Manufactured in the United States of America
1 2 3 4 5 6 – JR – 09 08 07 06 05 04

easy menu ethnic cookbooks

COOKING

revised and expanded

THE

to include new low-fat

AUSTRALIAN

and vegetarian recipes

WAY

Elizabeth Germaine & Ann L. Burckhardt

Ŀ Lerner Publications Company • Minneapolis

Contents

Introduction

When many people think of Australia, they picture a colorful, wild land full of dangerous crocodiles, cuddly koalas, and daring adventurers. In fact, Australia is a country of many different lifestyles and climates, ranging from the desolate outback—where neighbors live very far apart—to crowded coastal cities such as Sydney and Melbourne. In the tropical north, people can wear shorts year-round, while in the colder south they sometimes get the chance to ski on snowcapped mountains.

Australian cooking reflects this variety. It combines the foods of Britain—the homeland of Australian colonists—with foods brought by southern European immigrants and, more recently, by immigrants from neighboring countries near the Pacific Ocean. Creative Australian cooks adapt the ever-widening range of influences and fresh produce to their busy schedules.

Australia's British heritage is reflected in the custom of serving afternoon tea. Tomato and mint sandwiches are often served at teatime. (Recipe on page 39.)

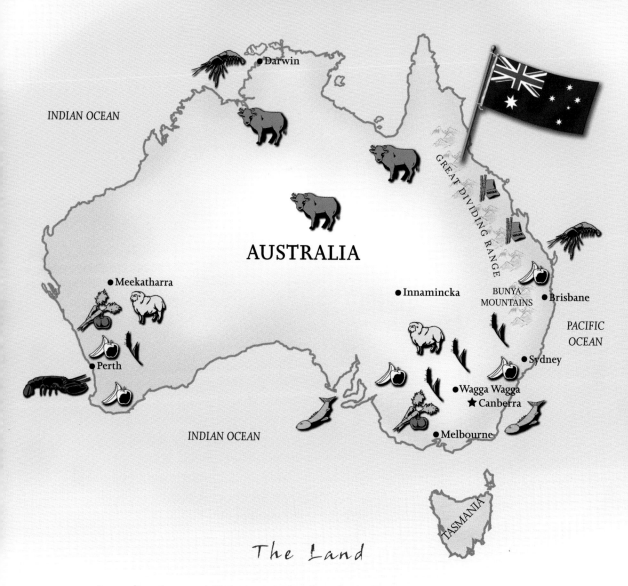

INDIAN OCEAN

Darwin

AUSTRALIA

Meekatharra

Perth

INDIAN OCEAN

Innamincka

BUNYA MOUNTAINS

Brisbane

PACIFIC OCEAN

Sydney

Wagga Wagga

★ Canberra

Melbourne

GREAT DIVIDING RANGE

TASMANIA

The Land

Australia, the world's biggest island and smallest continent, is called "down under" because it lies entirely within the Southern Hemisphere—south of the equator. Australia also includes the island of Tasmania, which lies south of Melbourne. The waters of the Indian and Pacific Oceans lap Australia's shores. The island of New Guinea lies to the north, and New Zealand is to the southeast. Australia is part of the group of countries called the Pacific Rim.

This island continent covers nearly three million square miles, roughly the size of the mainland United States. Australia is home to 19.7 million people, who are nicknamed Aussies. The nation's capital is Canberra.

A sparsely populated desert occupies the central part of this vast land, and the mountains of the Great Dividing Range run down the eastern coast. Bustling cities and sparkling beaches line the eastern, southeastern, and extreme southwestern coasts. Fertile farms and large ranches, called stations, lie in the nation's rural areas.

Because Australia lies in the Southern Hemisphere, its seasons are the reverse of those in the Northern Hemisphere. The coolest winter months are between June and August, while summer's heat lasts from December to February. In general, Australia has a warm, dry, pleasant climate, but the climate varies from one part of the country to another. Tourists generally visit the hot, tropical northern areas during the dry winter season. Rain comes to the north during the hot summer months—and when it rains, it pours. The climate of the southeast is milder, and most of the region's rain falls during the winter months. Although it does not snow in any of the large southeastern cities, snow does fall in the nearby mountains.

In addition to having a variety of climates, Australia is also home to some very unique wildlife. For example, the kangaroo and the koala are marsupials—mammals that give birth to helpless offspring

Wild kangaroos hop around many parts of Australia's rugged outback area.

9

that mature in a pouch on their mother's abdomen. Other native animals include the emu (an ostrichlike, flightless bird), the duck-billed platypus, and the laughing kookaburra bird with its unique call. The kangaroo and the emu are depicted on the national coat of arms.

The History

Place names such as Meekatharra, Innamincka, Oodnadatta, and Wagga Wagga dot the Australian map. These colorful names were used by the aborigines, nomadic people who have inhabited Australia for at least forty thousand years. An important part of the aborigines' culture is the idea of the Dreamtime. Aborigines believe that the first beings on earth lived during the Dreamtime. According to aboriginal legends, these first inhabitants were spirits who created natural wonders such as fire, rain, and land formations. The Dreamtime spirits told tales that guided daily life, from fishing and hunting to finding shelter. From these stories, the aborigines learned how to live in Australia's environment, which was very dry and sometimes harsh.

Modern Australian history dates to January 1788, when Europeans first landed just north of Botany Bay—later named Sydney Harbor. At that time, Britain imprisoned many people for fairly minor crimes, such as being unable to pay debts. As a result, British prisons were badly overcrowded. To solve the problem, the British government created a colony in Australia. About seven hundred prisoners and two hundred British soldiers—some with wives and children—established the first European settlement in what became the city of Sydney.

These colonists survived with basic supplies and food staples from Britain, supplemented by the food they found around them—fish, wild fruits, and nuts. But living conditions were harsh. The Australian climate was hot and dry compared to the cool, rainy British Isles.

The Irish potato famine, a crop failure that began in 1845 and

Ayers Rock, called Uluru by the aborigines, has cultural and spiritual significance for the area's native Australians. Ancient paintings on the rock depict scenes related to the Dreamtime.

during which thousands of Irish people starved to death or fled Ireland, prompted a flood of Irish immigration to Australia. In 1851, when gold was discovered in southern Australia, thousands more immigrants from various nations headed to the island. Many prospectors who did not find gold stayed in Australia, bought plots of land, and became farmers. After World War II (1939–1945), large numbers of Italians, Greeks, and other Europeans moved down under. Later, many families from Southeast Asia arrived to work and live in Australia.

Because of Australia's historic ties to Britain, Australian culture shares similarities with British culture. Many Aussies have a special affection for Britain.

But this connection with Britain meant that, for a long time, Australians did not have a national identity of their own. They bought goods and borrowed customs from other countries, chiefly Britain and the United States. Over the years, however, Aussies have gradually developed a sense of national pride in their unique island home.

The Food

The aborigines were experts at using the fresh, natural foods of their native land. Fruits, seeds, nuts, vegetables, and flower nectars all had their places on aboriginal menus, alongside seafood, meat such as kangaroo or possum, and various insects.

Later, rural Australians—who were known as bushmen because they lived in the Australian wilderness, which is also known as the outback or the bush—ate hearty, simple food that they called "tucker." Bushmen usually carried a tucker bag containing some flour, from which they made a simple bread called *damper*. Though damper was nothing but a flour-and-water dough cooked on a stick held over the campfire or baked in the ashes, to hungry bushmen, it was delicious.

Modern Australian cooking is built on a solid foundation of British cooking, part of the island-nation's colonial heritage. At one time, meat was the mainstay of the down-under diet. Because of the many ranches in Australia, meat was plentiful and excellent. Most families ate meat and potatoes at nearly every meal. Cooks usually served mutton (sheep meat) or lamb and sometimes beef or pork.

Two foods that most Australians love are meat pies and Vegemite. Meat pies—pastry crusts filled with meat and gravy—are tasty but high-fat snacks. Vegemite, on the other hand, is very healthy. A salty, black yeast extract, Vegemite is rich in vitamins and minerals. Aussies enjoy it spread ever-so-thinly on bread, toast, or rusks (very dry, crispy pieces of bread), and it is often one of a child's first solid foods.

But Australian cuisine has expanded beyond these traditional favorites. Since World War II, Australia has welcomed many immigrants. As a result of the multicultural influences of new ethnic groups, Australian menus have become more diverse. Italians and Greeks introduced squid and mussels, new vegetables, and various herbs. European cheese makers brought with them methods of making a wide range of fine cheeses from cow and goat milk. Vietnamese and Chinese immigrants introduced stir-fries and sold special ingredients such as ginger, vegetables, greens, and hot peppers.

A shop in a Melbourne market sells cheeses from Australia and Europe.

Australian diners enjoy access to many kinds of fish. A seafood vendor shows off the catch of the day.

No matter what the style of cooking, seafood that has been freshly caught along Australia's long shoreline is superb. Diners can select prawns (large shrimp), lobsters, scallops, or fillets from dozens of species of fish.

Fruits and vegetables arrive fresh in Aussie kitchens, too. The populous southeast corner of the country contains many orchards, vineyards, and farm gardens. Australian cooks also enjoy preparing baked goods, and they often use hearty whole-grain flours for their breads and sweets.

Holidays and Festivals

Just as Australian cooking is a combination of tradition and experiment, holidays in Australia bring together new and old customs. Before the arrival of Europeans, Australia's aborigines had their own set of beliefs and rituals. Later, most of the British colonists and settlers were Christian, and the majority of modern-day Australians follow one of the branches of Christianity. For them, Christmas, on December 25, is one of the year's biggest holidays.

Because Australia lies in the Southern Hemisphere, Christmas falls right in the middle of summer. Kids are on a six-week vacation, the beaches are packed, and many people are busy shopping for holiday gifts and making preparations. Although some families have Christmas trees, wintry decorations such as pine boughs and holly are often replaced by native Australian plants. Christmas bells, a brightly colored flower with bell-shaped blossoms, and branches of the Christmas bush, a flowering tree, adorn many Australian homes. On Christmas Eve, the pleasant weather allows Melbourne residents to hold the Carols by Candlelight celebration outdoors. For more than sixty years, Aussies of every age have gathered to sing Christmas carols at this annual event.

Christmas Day is usually hot in Australia—temperatures sometimes soar higher than 100°F. Even in such steamy weather, some Australians prepare traditional Christmas dinners, often heavily influenced by British custom. These dinners include dishes such as roast turkey, ham, potatoes with gravy, and cooked vegetables. However, many people have adopted newer, more summery traditions, and Christmas picnics and backyard barbecues are popular. Cold roasts, such as turkey, ham, or roast beef, or grilled foods, such as fish, shrimp, chicken, or vegetables, accompany salads and fruit dishes. Desserts are also a must, with favorites including light, airy pavlova— a meringue pastry topped with fresh fruit and whipped cream— Christmas pudding, shortbread, and bonbons.

After dinner, children and their families enjoy trips to the seaside or to the park to play with new toys and to visit with friends. December 26, which is the national holiday Boxing Day, gives people a chance to relax and clean up after the festivities.

Another big day is January 26, Australia Day. This holiday commemorates the official founding of a British colony in Australia. Throughout the nation, parades, fireworks, live entertainment, and craft fairs celebrate Australian history and culture. In Sydney, hungry revelers can get their fill at the Great Australian Bite, a giant food festival. Many cities and towns hold community breakfasts, serving up bacon, eggs, and pancakes to get the day off to a good start. Events such as log-chopping contests and campfire cooking competitions test Australians' skills in the outback.

Not long after Australia Day, an event with even older roots takes place in the Bunya Mountains, located northwest of the eastern city of Brisbane. Australia's aboriginal residents hold many ceremonies and rituals, called corroborees. Most of these occasions are very sacred, and their details are kept private within individual aboriginal communities. However, aborigines from many different groups shared the ancient Bunya Festival. Long before the British colonists arrived, aborigines from around the region met in the Bunya Mountains every few years to enjoy corroborees and feasts. The festival took place in late January or early February, during the harvest season of bunya nuts. Bunya nuts are large seeds produced by the bunya pine trees that flourish in the mountains, and festivalgoers sampled various dishes prepared with the nuts. In recent years, the Bunya Festival has been revived and celebrated in modern Australia.

Another unique Australian celebration is shearing time. Each September—early spring in Australia—the many sheep raised on Australian farms and ranches get their annual haircut. Their wool is sheared off and used to make clothing and other goods. When the shearing—which often takes several days—is finished, rural families celebrate with a big picnic by the billabong, a waterhole formed by a river or creek. Kids swim in the cool water, while adults tend the

Farm workers in Tasmania herd their sheep. Sheep's wool is an important product for Australia, and the annual shearing is a big event.

cooking fire. The firewood is often eucalyptus, also called gum, or *coolabah*. Native to Australia, the wood gives off a nose-tingling aroma as it burns.

Common dishes at these springtime picnics include grilled lamb chops, bread and butter, salad, and three or four kinds of biscuits and cakes. As the sun sets after the evening picnic, full, tired diners listen to the black-crested cockatoos calling overhead and the kookaburras laughing in the trees. Shearing time in the outback is a truly Australian experience.

Before You Begin

Australian cooking makes use of some ingredients that you may not know. Sometimes special cookware is used, too, although the recipes in this book can be prepared with ordinary utensils and pans.

The most important thing you need to know before you start is how to be a careful cook. On the following page, you'll find a few rules that will make your cooking experience safe, fun, and easy. Next, take a look at the "dictionary" of utensils, terms, and special ingredients. You may also want to read the list of tips on preparing healthy, low-fat meals.

When you've picked out a recipe to try, read through it from beginning to end. Now you are ready to shop for ingredients and to organize the cookware you will need. Once you have assembled everything, you're ready to begin cooking.

Pavlova, a popular Australian dessert, can be topped with fruits that grow in Australia, such as kiwifruit, strawberries, or bananas. (Recipe on pages 66–67.)

The Careful Cook

Whenever you cook, there are certain safety rules you must always keep in mind. Even experienced cooks follow these rules when they are in the kitchen.

- Always wash your hands before handling food. Thoroughly wash all raw vegetables and fruits to remove dirt, chemicals, and insecticides. Wash uncooked poultry, fish, and meat under cold water.
- Use a cutting board when cutting up vegetables and fruits. Don't cut them up in your hand! And be sure to cut in a direction *away* from you and your fingers.
- Long hair or loose clothing can easily catch fire if brought near the burners of a stove. If you have long hair, tie it back before you start cooking.
- Turn all pot handles toward the back of the stove so that you will not catch your sleeves or jewelry on them. This is especially important when younger brothers and sisters are around. They could easily knock off a pot and get burned.
- Always use a pot holder to steady hot pots or to take pans out of the oven. Don't use a wet cloth on a hot pan because the steam it produces could burn you.
- Lift the lid of a steaming pot with the opening away from you so that you will not get burned.
- If you get burned, hold the burn under cold running water. Do not put grease or butter on it. Cold water helps to take the heat out, but grease or butter will only keep it in.
- If grease or cooking oil catches fire, throw baking soda or salt at the bottom of the flame to put it out. (Water will *not* put out a grease fire.) Call for help, and try to turn all the stove burners to "off."

Cooking Utensils

electric mixer—An appliance, either freestanding or handheld, used for mixing and beating

food processor—An electric appliance with a container and rotating blade to chop, mix, and blend food

kitchen parchment paper—A nonstick pan liner

kitchen shears—Scissors designed especially to snip herbs and cut a wide variety of other foods

meat thermometer—A thermometer that is inserted into meat or poultry to check how well-done the meat is. Some meat thermometers are left in the whole time the meat cooks, while others are used at intervals.

paring knife—A small knife used for removing pits and cores from fruit and for peeling vegetables and fruit

pastry brush—A small brush used for coating food or cooking equipment with melted butter or other liquids

rack—A metal frame on which meat is placed for roasting

rolling pin—A cylinder, often of wood, used for rolling out pastry or dough

serrated knife—A knife with a notched or grooved cutting edge

spatula—A flat, thin utensil used to lift, toss, turn, or scoop up food

tongs—A utensil, shaped either like tweezers or scissors with flat, blunt ends, used to grasp food

wire rack—An open wire stand on which hot food is cooled

wire wisk—A utensil used for beating food by hand

Cooking Terms

beat—To stir rapidly in a circular motion

boil—To heat a liquid over high heat until bubbles form and rise rapidly to the surface chop—To cut into small pieces

core—To remove the seeds or pit from the center of a fruit or vegetable

cut in—To mix butter or margarine into flour with a pastry blender or two knives until it has a coarse, mealy texture

dollop—A small amount, about a teaspoonful, of a semiliquid ingredient such as whipped cream

fillet—A boneless piece of fish or meat

garnish—To decorate a dish with small pieces of food, such as parsley sprigs

mince—To chop food into very small pieces

pinch—A very small amount, usually what you can pick up between your thumb and first finger

roast—To cook in an open pan in an oven

sift—To put an ingredient, such as powdered sugar, through a sifter to break up any lumps

simmer—To cook over low heat in liquid kept just below boiling point. Bubbles will occasionally rise to the surface.

whip—To beat ingredients at a high speed until mixture is light and fluffy

Special Ingredients

chutney—A thick sauce made from fruit, spices, and vinegar or lemon juice

cinnamon—A spice made from the bark of a tree in the laurel family. Cinnamon is available ground or in sticks.

curry powder—A blend of six or more herbs, seeds, and spices that gives food a spicy flavor and a yellow hue

dry mustard—A powder made from the ground seeds of the mustard plant that is used to flavor food

garlic—A bulbous herb whose distinctive flavor is used in many dishes. Each piece or bulb can be broken up into several small sections called cloves. Before chopping a clove of garlic, remove its papery skin.

gingerroot—The knobby, light brown root of a tropical plant, used to flavor food. To use fresh gingerroot, slice off the amount called for, peel off the skin with the side of a spoon, and grate the flesh. Freeze the rest of the root for future use. Fresh ginger has a very zippy taste, so use it sparingly. (Do not substitute dried ground ginger in a recipe calling for fresh ginger, as the taste is very different.)

kiwifruit—A small oval fruit with fuzzy brown skin and bright green flesh marked with a circle of tiny black seeds

mint—The leaves of any of a variety of mint plants, used fresh or dried in cooking

nutmeg—A fragrant spice, either whole or ground, that is often used in desserts

olive oil—An oil made from pressed olives that is used in cooking and for dressing salads

parsley—A green, leafy herb used as a seasoning and as a garnish

parsnip—A white root vegetable with a mild, slightly sweet, nutty flavor

passion fruit—A small, egg-shaped fruit with a hard purple shell protecting yellow-orange pulp, which has a tart-sweet flavor. It is more readily available canned than fresh in the United States.

rosemary—An herb in the mint family. Rosemary's needlelike leaves have a strong flavor and are used as a seasoning and as a garnish.

self-rising flour—Flour which already has baking powder and salt added to it. Australian cooks often use self-rising flour for convenience.

thyme—A fragrant herb used fresh or dry to season foods

wine vinegar—Vinegar made from red or white wine. Wine vinegars usually have a sharp, tangy flavor.

Healthy and Low-Fat Cooking Tips

Many modern cooks are concerned about preparing healthy, low-fat meals. Fortunately, there are simple ways to reduce the fat content of most dishes. Here are a few general tips for adapting the recipes in this book. Throughout the book, you'll also find specific suggestions for individual recipes—and don't worry, they'll still taste delicious!

Many recipes call for butter or oil to sauté vegetables or other ingredients. Using oil instead of butter can lower cholesterol and saturated fat, but you can also reduce the amount of oil you use or use a low-fat or nonfat cooking spray instead of oil. Sprinkling a little salt on vegetables brings out their natural juices, so less oil is needed. It's also a good idea to use a small, nonstick frying pan if you decide to use less oil than the recipe calls for.

Another common substitution for butter is margarine. Before making this substitution, consider the recipe. If it is a dessert, it's often best to use butter. Margarine may noticeably change the taste or consistency of the food.

Other dairy products, such as heavy cream, milk, and sour cream, also show up in Australian cooking. An easy way to trim fat from a recipe is to use skim or evaporated skim milk in place of cream, whole milk, or 2 percent milk. In recipes that call for sour cream, you may want to try substituting low-fat or nonfat varieties, or plain yogurt. When cooking with meat, buying extra-lean meats and trimming off as much fat as possible are two simple ways to reduce fat.

There are many ways to prepare meals that are good for you and still taste great. As you become a more experienced cook, try experimenting with recipes and substitutions to find the methods that work best for you.

METRIC CONVERSIONS

Cooks in the United States measure both liquid and solid ingredients using standard containers based on the 8-ounce cup and the tablespoon. These measurements are based on volume, while the metric system of measurement is based on both weight (for solids) and volume (for liquids). To convert from U.S. fluid tablespoons, ounces, quarts, and so forth to metric liters is a straightforward conversion, using the chart below. However, since solids have different weights—one cup of rice does not weigh the same as one cup of grated cheese, for example—many cooks who use the metric system have kitchen scales to weigh different ingredients. The chart below will give you a good starting point for basic conversions to the metric system.

MASS (weight)

1 ounce (oz.)	=	28.0 grams (g)
8 ounces	=	227.0 grams
1 pound (lb.) or 16 ounces	=	0.45 kilograms (kg)
2.2 pounds	=	1.0 kilogram

LIQUID VOLUME

1 teaspoon (tsp.)	=	5.0 milliliters (ml)
1 tablespoon (tbsp.)	=	15.0 milliliters
1 fluid ounce (oz.)	=	30.0 milliliters
1 cup (c.)	=	240 milliliters
1 pint (pt.)	=	480 milliliters
1 quart (qt.)	=	0.95 liters (l)
1 gallon (gal.)	=	3.80 liters

LENGTH

¼ inch (in.)	=	0.6 centimeters (cm)
½ inch	=	1.25 centimeters
1 inch	=	2.5 centimeters

TEMPERATURE

212°F	=	100°C (boiling point of water)
225°F	=	110°C
250°F	=	120°C
275°F	=	135°C
300°F	=	150°C
325°F	=	160°C
350°F	=	180°C
375°F	=	190°C
400°F	=	200°C

(To convert temperature in Fahrenheit to Celsius, subtract 32 and multiply by .56)

PAN SIZES

8-inch cake pan	=	20 x 4-centimeter cake pan
9-inch cake pan	=	23 x 3.5-centimeter cake pan
11 x 7-inch baking pan	=	28 x 18-centimeter baking pan
13 x 9-inch baking pan	=	32.5 x 23-centimeter baking pan
9 x 5-inch loaf pan	=	23 x 13-centimeter loaf pan
2-quart casserole	=	2-liter casserole

An Australian Table

Many Australian families gather for meals at dinner tables in their kitchens or dining rooms. In busy households, the evening meal can be a good time to slow down and share news and stories about the day.

But perhaps one of the most typically Australian places to eat is not in the dining room or the kitchen but in the backyard or at a local park. Barbecues and cookouts are favorite gatherings for Aussies of all ages. And, with warm weather lasting through most of the year in much of the country, barbecues are not just summertime treats.

An Australian barbecue is usually a casual, fun event for families and friends. Maybe you've heard people say, "Throw another shrimp on the barbie." This expression turns up in movies more often than in real life, but the "barbie" is the grill, and large shrimp (also called prawns) are popular at barbecues. Fish and other types of seafood are also common foods at cookouts, especially near Australia's coastal waters. Other tasty dishes from the grill might include lamb chops, sausages, roasted eggplant, or even marinated pears. So to experience one kind of eating the Australian way, invite some friends over and start up the barbie!

Hikers in a park near Brisbane fire up the barbie for a picnic.

An Australian Menu

The following menus are examples of a typical Australian lunch and dinner. Shopping lists of the ingredients necessary to prepare these meals are also included. Keep in mind that these combinations of dishes are just suggestions. You can make your own menu plans based on the available ingredients, the occasion, and the amount of time that you have to prepare.

LUNCH

Egg and bacon pie

Fresh fruit salad

Lamingtons

SHOPPING LIST:

Produce

1 to 1½ lb. fresh fruit of your choice
fresh parsley or chives

Dairy/Egg/Meat

1 stick butter or margarine
6 eggs
8 thin slices Canadian bacon

Canned/Bottled/Boxed

1 18½-oz. package yellow cake mix

Miscellaneous

1 17½-oz. package frozen puff pastry sheets (2 sheets)
cocoa
3 c. shredded coconut
powdered sugar
salt
black pepper

DINNER

Creamy pumpkin soup

Sunshine salad with vinaigrette dressing

Crunchy fish fillets

Bread and butter custard

SHOPPING LIST:

Produce

1 large yellow onion
1 small red onion (optional)
1 small head lettuce
1 small cucumber
1 banana
1 lemon
fresh parsley

Dairy/Egg/Meat

2 sticks butter
16 oz. half-and-half, whole milk, or fat free half-and-half
8 oz. milk
8 oz. heavy cream
8 oz. sour cream (regular, low-fat, or nonfat)
4 eggs
1 lb. white fish fillets (orange roughy, perch, or cod)

Canned/Bottled/Boxed

1 15-oz. can pumpkin
2 10¾-oz. cans chicken or vegetable broth
1 11-oz. can mandarin orange segments
olive oil
vegetable oil
wine vinegar
tartar sauce
lemon juice
vanilla extract
2½ c. rolled oats

Miscellaneous

4 slices white bread
½ c. golden raisins
all-purpose flour
sugar
curry powder
dry mustard
cinnamon
nutmeg
salt
black pepper

Lunch

Although Australian breakfasts were once very substantial meals, this is no longer true for most Aussies. People who work on farms or do other physically demanding jobs may still eat a hearty breakfast of eggs, bacon, cooked tomato, and toast. However, most modern Australians eat a light breakfast of cereal, fresh fruit, and milk or orange juice.

Lunch, too, is often a relatively light meal. A sandwich, a couple of biscuits (cookies) or a piece of cake, fresh fruit, and a drink make up a filling and delicious lunch. Busy Aussies might also stop to enjoy a hot meat pie with ketchup.

On weekends Australians love to go on picnics. They either barbecue the main course at an outdoor grill or prepare something like a quiche or other entrée ahead of time to take along. They may also bring a salad and bread or rolls. Something sweet usually follows the main course.

Egg and bacon pie is one of the many kinds of hearty meat pies that Australians enjoy for lunch. (Recipe on page 32.)

Egg and Bacon Pie

1 17½-oz. package frozen puff
   pastry sheets, thawed (2 sheets)*

8 thin slices Canadian bacon

6 eggs

¼ tsp. salt

⅛ tsp. pepper

¼ c. finely chopped parsley or
   chives

*Homemade puff pastry is delicious but
difficult and time consuming to make.
The ready-made sheets are convenient to use
and are just as tasty when baked. Be sure to
thaw sheets at room temperature for at least
20 minutes before using. If the pastry starts
to crack while you're working with it, just
wet your fingers with a little water and
press the pastry firmly together to seal.*

1. Preheat oven to 400°F. On a lightly floured working surface, use a rolling pin to roll out one sheet of pastry until it is ⅛-inch thick.

2. Line a 9-inch pie plate with pastry sheet and press gently into place. Cover pastry with Canadian bacon, overlapping slices to form an even layer. Crack eggs onto bacon-lined crust and break yolks with a fork. Season with salt and pepper and sprinkle with parsley or chives.

3. Roll out the second sheet of pastry to ⅛-inch thick. With your fingers or a pastry brush, lightly brush the lower pastry's edge with water. Gently place the second sheet of pastry on top of the pie. Press edges firmly together and cut off any extra pastry. Flute edges by pinching pastry gently between your thumb and forefinger. Carefully use a sharp knife to cut a few small slits in the middle of the top crust.

4. Place pie plate on a baking sheet and bake for 30 minutes, or until pastry is puffed and golden brown. Carefully remove pie from the oven and allow to cool before serving.

Preparation time: 25 to 30 minutes
Baking time: 30 minutes
Serves 6

Fresh Fruit Salad

The beauty of fruit salad is that you can use your imagination! It can be made with almost any combination of fruits that are in season. In Australia passion fruit is a common ingredient. Select three or four of your favorite fruits.

About 1 to 1½ lb. fresh fruit, such as apricots, bananas, strawberries, peaches, pears, apples, oranges, grapes, or melon

1. Wash fruit thoroughly. Peel, core, and remove the stones or pits as necessary. Cut the fruit into small chunks or bite-sized pieces.

2. Combine the fruit in a bowl.* Stir gently, being careful not to bruise or mash the fruit. Cover and chill until ready to serve.

Preparation time: 15 to 20 minutes
Serves 4

If you like your salad extra sweet, add 2 tbsp. sugar to the fruit and stir gently.

Pineapple Fruit Cup

Many Australian families like to serve refreshing fruit drinks like this one for celebrations or on hot afternoons.

4 c. pineapple juice

2 c. apricot nectar

1 c. orange juice

4 c. lemon-lime soda or club soda

4 c. ginger ale

1 apple

mint sprigs for garnish

1. Chill fruit juices, soda, and ginger ale ahead of time.

2. Peel, core, and finely chop the apple.

3. Measure pineapple juice, apricot nectar, and orange juice into a large pitcher or 1-gallon jug. Add chopped apple and stir well to mix.

4. Add soda and ginger ale just before serving. Pour into ice-filled glasses and garnish each fruit cup with a sprig of mint.

Preparation time: 10 to 15 minutes
Serves 10 to 12

*For an extra burst of color and flavor, stir in 4 oz. candied cherries, cut into quarters.

Afternoon Tea

Tea is one of the most common beverages in Australia. Aussie children develop a taste for tea by sipping a little bit of it mixed with lots of milk and sugar. Australians may enjoy a "cuppa"—a cup of tea—at any time of the day, but in the morning and afternoon it is usually accompanied by a snack. Morning tea—a cup of tea or coffee served with a biscuit or a scone—is lighter than afternoon tea.

The custom of having afternoon tea at 4:00 P.M. each day came to Australia from England, and it can be quite a formal occasion. Tea is served with a selection of sandwiches, scones, cookies, and cakes—both elaborate and plain. Although most modern Australians lead busy lives, the tradition of afternoon tea lives on.

Australians drink tea at all hours of the day, but having afternoon tea with a variety of snacks is often a special event. (Recipe on page 38.)

Tea

The most traditional Australian tea was "billy tea." Brewed by bushmen in Australia's wilderness, the water was boiled and the tea was steeped in a metal container called a billy. Billy Tea is now a brand name of a popular Australian black tea. If you can't get Billy Tea, try other black teas such as English Breakfast in the morning and Earl Grey in the afternoon.

1 c. water per person

1 tsp. loose tea for each person plus one more tsp., or 1 tea bag for each person plus one more*

1. Place cold water in a kettle (not a teapot). Bring water to a boil.

2. Meanwhile, warm a teapot by filling it with hot tap water.

3. When water in the kettle boils, empty hot tap water from the teapot. Place tea in teapot.

4. Fill teapot with the boiling water.

5. Allow tea to steep (soak) for 2 minutes and serve hot.

Preparation time: 12 to 14 minutes

*Most Australians like the taste of their tea to be quite strong. The extra teaspoonful or tea bag is called "one for the pot," and it gives the tea the extra flavor that Aussies love.

Tomato and Mint Sandwiches

These triangular sandwiches are tasty tidbits to snack on at teatime. They are not meant to fill you up, since dinner is usually not too far off.

4 thin slices white or whole wheat bread

1 to 2 tbsp. soft butter or margarine

1 tomato*

dash salt and pepper

⅛ tsp. sugar

several sprigs fresh mint

*For a variation on this recipe, use thinly sliced, peeled cucumber in place of the tomato and leave out the sugar.

1. Trim crusts from bread.

2. Spread softened butter or margarine thinly on bread. (This will keep the tomatoes from making the bread soggy.)

3. Cut tomato into thin slices. Using a serrated knife will make cutting the tomato easier.

4. Place tomato slices on two of the buttered bread slices. Sprinkle tomato slices with salt, pepper, and sugar.

5. Wash mint and dry the sprigs between paper towels. With kitchen shears, snip mint leaves from 2 sprigs into tiny pieces and sprinkle them over the tomato slices.

6. Cover tomato slices with remaining slices of bread. Cut each sandwich into four triangular pieces. Arrange sandwiches on a plate or small platter and garnish with extra sprigs of mint. Refrigerate until serving.

Preparation time: 20 minutes
Serves 4

Anzac Biscuits

These sweet biscuits are named for the Australian and New Zealand Army Corps (ANZAC), which fought in World War I (1914–1918).

1 c. rolled oats

¾ c. unsweetened shredded coconut

1 c. all-purpose flour

1 c. sugar

½ c. butter or margarine

1 tbsp. honey or light corn syrup

1½ tsp. baking soda

2 tbsp. boiling water

1. Preheat oven to 300°F.

2. Measure the oats, coconut, flour, and sugar into a medium-sized mixing bowl. Stir well.

3. In a small pan over medium-low heat, melt butter or margarine and stir in honey or corn syrup.

4. Place baking soda in a cup or small bowl. Pour boiling water over baking soda and stir to dissolve. Add to melted butter mixture.

5. Pour butter mixture over oat mixture. Mix well.

6. Cover two baking sheets with kitchen parchment paper or aluminum foil (dull side up). Drop teaspoonfuls of dough 2 inches apart onto sheets.

7. Bake 10 to 12 minutes, or until biscuits spread and are evenly browned.

8. Cool biscuits on a baking sheet for 1 to 2 minutes. Remove with a spatula and finish cooling on wire racks.

Preparation time: 30 to 35 minutes
Baking time: 10 to 12 minutes
Makes about 4 dozen biscuits

Dinner

Dinner is usually the largest meal of the day in Australian homes. The meal generally has more courses than lunch, and sometimes the foods are heavier or richer than those served at the midday meal.

Soup or another light dish may be served as a first course for dinner. The meal's main entrée is usually meat or fish, and this is still true in many homes. However, main dishes such as beef curry reflect Australia's diverse heritage. In modern Australia, vegetarian meals are also becoming more popular. Whatever the entrée may be, it is often served with cooked vegetables or with a salad. Sometimes salad is served as a separate course after the entrée, but it is almost never served before the main course, as it frequently is in the United States.

Much like Australia itself, beef curry has both British and Indian influences. (Recipe on pages 48–49.)

Creamy Pumpkin Soup

Nearly every Australian family has its own version of this delicious golden soup. Prepare it on a chilly autumn evening for a warming treat.

¼ c. butter or margarine*

I large yellow onion, peeled and chopped

½ tsp. curry powder

I 15-oz. can pumpkin

¼ tsp. salt

2 c. half-and-half*

2½ c. chicken or vegetable broth

⅛ tsp. cinnamon

2 tsp. minced parsley

⅓ c. sour cream*

1. Melt butter in a medium-sized saucepan. Add chopped onion and cook, stirring frequently, until onion is soft but not brown. Add curry powder and cook 1 to 2 minutes longer.

2. Place curried onion in a food processor or blender. Add pumpkin and salt and process until smooth. Add half-and-half and process again until smooth.

3. Pour pumpkin mixture back into saucepan and stir in chicken or vegetable broth. Heat soup slowly over low heat, stirring occasionally. Meanwhile, stir cinnamon and minced parsley into the sour cream.

4. Serve soup steaming hot with a dollop of seasoned sour cream atop each bowl.

Preparation time: 10 minutes
Cooking time: 15 minutes
Serves 6

*For a lighter soup, use half the amount of butter, evaporated skim milk instead of half-and-half, and low-fat or nonfat sour cream instead of regular.

Crunchy Fish Fillets

The waters around Australia abound in fish and shellfish, which are as delicious as their names are unique. Garfish, gemfish, leatherjacket, and snook are just a few examples. If you can't get any of these unusual varieties, choose fish such as orange roughy, perch, or cod for this tasty dish.

4 firm white fish fillets, fresh or
    frozen and thawed (about 1 lb.)

½ c. all-purpose flour

½ tsp. salt

¼ tsp. pepper

2 eggs

2½ c. rolled oats

¼ c. vegetable oil plus ¼ c.
    (½ stick) butter for frying

1 lemon, cut into wedges

bottled tartar sauce

1. Rinse fish under cold running water and pat dry with paper towels.

2. Place flour, salt, and pepper in a medium-sized plastic bag.

3. Beat eggs in a shallow bowl and place the bowl next to the bag of flour.

4. Place the oats in another shallow bowl alongside the eggs.

5. Put 1 or 2 fish fillets in the plastic bag and close it securely. Shake the bag gently until fish is coated with flour. Open bag, shake off excess flour, and remove fish.

6. Place the flour-coated fish in the bowl of beaten egg. Using two forks, turn the fillets to coat them completely. Let excess egg drip off.

7. Toss the egg-coated fish in the oats, coating completely. Arrange fillets on a plate in a single layer and chill until ready to fry. Meanwhile, line a plate or baking sheet with paper towels.

8. To fry, heat the oil and butter in a frying pan over medium-high heat until hot. Place fish fillets in the pan, being careful not to crowd them.*

9. Cook 3 to 4 minutes on each side, or until the oats are a deep, golden brown. Using a spatula, carefully remove fillets from the pan and drain them on the towel-lined plate.

10. Serve as soon as possible with a lemon wedge or tartar sauce. Chips (french fries) and salad are good accompaniments.

Preparation time: 25 minutes
Cooking time: 10 to 15 minutes
Serves 4

*To lower the amount of fat in this dish, you can bake the fillets rather than frying them. After coating fish with oats, place fillets on the bottom of a lightly greased baking dish or baking sheet. Drizzle 2 to 3 tbsp. melted butter over fish and bake, uncovered, in a 450°F oven for 12 minutes, or until fish flakes easily.

Beef Curry

Curry was originally an Indian dish. It became popular in Britain during the British colonization of India in the 1700s, and curry soon became a favorite in Australia as well. This dish is usually served with plain white rice and a variety of condiments for garnishing, such as peanuts, sliced bananas, golden or dark raisins, diced pineapple, sliced or chopped hard-boiled egg, and bottled chutney.

1½ lb. beef round steak cut into 1-inch cubes (Ask the butcher to do this for you or check your grocery store for beef that has already been cut up.)*

3 tbsp. vegetable oil

2 large onions, peeled and finely chopped

2 cloves garlic, peeled and crushed

2 tsp. finely chopped fresh gingerroot

1½ tbsp. curry powder

1 tsp. salt

1 large tomato, peeled and chopped

1½ c. canned beef stock

1 tbsp. soft butter

2 tbsp. flour

1. Use a sharp knife to trim any fat from steak. Place meat in a casserole dish.

2. Preheat oven to 350°F.

3. Heat oil in a large skillet over medium-high heat. Add onions, garlic, and gingerroot to the skillet and cook 2 to 3 minutes.

4. Stir in curry powder and cook another minute or two. Add salt, chopped tomato, and beef stock. Bring to a boil while stirring.

5. Pour the curry sauce over the beef. Cover the casserole with a lid or heavy-duty aluminum foil. Place in oven and bake for 1½ hours, or until very tender. (Instead of baking, you can also simmer the beef curry in a covered saucepan on the stove. Place saucepan over very low heat and cook for about 2 hours, or until beef is very tender.)

6. When the curry is almost done, place butter in a cup. Sprinkle 1 tbsp. flour over the butter. Using a wooden spoon, mix the flour into the butter, forming a paste. Then mix in the second tablespoon of flour.

7. Remove casserole dish from the oven. Carefully return curry to the skillet and place over medium heat. Add butter paste to curry a teaspoonful at a time. Cook, stirring constantly, until liquid thickens.

8. Serve with rice and a selection of condiments.

Preparation time: 15 to 20 minutes
Cooking time: 1¾ to 2 hours
Serves 5 to 6

*For a delicious vegetarian curry, replace the beef with 1½ lb. potatoes, cut into chunks, and replace beef stock with vegetable broth. You might also want to try adding other vegetables, such as peas, carrots, and cauliflower. Omitting meat will reduce your cooking time, as well. Bake until vegetables are tender, about 20 to 25 minutes.

Sunshine Salad with Vinaigrette Dressing

Australians frequently mix fruits and vegetables together in salads. The fresh flavor of this zesty combination is sure to delight your taste buds.

Vinaigrette dressing:

7 tbsp. olive oil or vegetable oil

2 tbsp. wine vinegar

⅛ tsp. salt

¼ tsp. dry mustard

pinch of pepper

Salad:

1 small head of lettuce, washed and dried

1 small cucumber, peeled and thinly sliced

1 11-oz. can mandarin orange segments, drained

¼ red onion, peeled and thinly sliced (optional)

1 banana

2 tsp. lemon juice

1. Place all dressing ingredients in a screw-top jar. Cover and shake vigorously for 30 seconds to mix thoroughly. Set dressing aside.

2. Tear lettuce into bite-sized pieces. Place in a salad bowl and add cucumber, mandarin orange segments, and red onion.

3. Slice banana and sprinkle it with lemon juice to prevent it from turning brown. Add banana to salad bowl. Cover and chill until ready to serve.

4. At serving time, toss salad with vinaigrette dressing.

Preparation time: 10 to 15 minutes
Serves 4 to 6

Desserts

Most daily Australian meals end with simple desserts. Australian cooks take advantage of the abundance of fresh fruit available, creating colorful fruit salads, stewed fruit dishes, and other treats. The passion fruit is one of the Aussies' favorite tropical fruits. Other popular choices are bananas and strawberries.

But in addition to delectable fresh fruit, richer desserts are also popular in Australia, particularly for special occasions. Favorite sweets include pies, cakes, and cookies. Sometimes these last courses also use native Australian fruits and other ingredients. For example, the glazed kiwi tart makes good use of the delicious green kiwifruit that flourishes in Australia and New Zealand. Whether dessert is slices of fresh fruit or a bowl of rich bread and butter custard, an Australian meal always ends on a sweet note.

The kiwifruit that tops this colorful tart hides a delicious cream cheese filling. (Recipe on page 54.)

Glazed Kiwi Tart

Named for the kiwi bird of New Zealand, the kiwifruit has a delicious, mixed-fruit flavor and is high in vitamin C.

Pastry:

1 9-in. unbaked pie shell (look for this in the refrigerated section of your grocery store or supermarket)

Filling:

1 8-oz. package cream cheese, at room temperature*

⅔ c. sugar

1½ tsp. vanilla extract

3 tbsp. heavy cream*

3 ripe kiwifruit

Glaze:

¼ c. apricot preserves

1 tbsp. water

1. To make the pie shell, follow the directions on the package for a one-crust pie. Use a fork to thoroughly prick the bottom and sides of the pastry shell and bake pastry according to package directions.

2. For the filling, combine cream cheese, sugar, vanilla, and heavy cream. Stir until smooth. Spread cream cheese filling in cooled pastry shell.

3. Peel kiwifruit with a paring knife and cut into thin slices. Arrange slices on top of cream cheese filling, overlapping them in circles.

4. To make glaze, combine apricot preserves and water in a small saucepan and heat until preserves melt. Cool slightly, stirring occasionally. Spoon glaze over kiwifruit and chill tart until ready to serve.

Preparation time: 25 minutes
(plus baking and cooling time for pastry shell)
Serves 6 to 8

*To reduce the fat content of this rich tart, use low-fat or nonfat cream cheese instead of regular cream cheese, and replace the heavy cream with evaporated skim milk or fat free half-and-half.

Lamingtons

These cakes are named after Baroness Lamington, wife of the governor of an Australian state at the beginning of the 1900s. Lamingtons are still a favorite with Australian children.

Cake:

1 18½-oz. package yellow cake mix

Icing:

3 c. powdered sugar

⅓ c. cocoa

3 tbsp. butter or margarine, melted

½ c. boiling water

3 c. shredded coconut

1. Bake cake as directed on the package for a 9 x 13-inch cake. When cake is cool, cut it into twelve pieces, about 2½ inches square each.

2. To make icing, sift powdered sugar and cocoa into a bowl. Add melted butter and boiling water and mix until smooth.

3. Place the bowl of icing in a pan one-quarter full of simmering water.

4. Place coconut in a shallow bowl next to saucepan. Place a wire rack on the other side of the coconut to form a lamington assembly line.

5. Using forks or tongs, dip a cake square into the hot icing. Turn to coat well and let excess icing drip off. Next, place icing-covered cake in the coconut. Roll cake in coconut to cover on all sides. Place the lamington on the wire rack and repeat with remaining pieces of cake. When all lamingtons are iced, put them in a cool place until the icing hardens.

Preparation time: 35 minutes
Baking time: 45 minutes
Makes 12 lamingtons

Bread and Butter Custard

This "comfort" food, once found only in the kitchens of Australian grandmothers, is now served in fine restaurants.

I to 2 tbsp. soft butter

4 slices white bread

½ c. golden raisins

2 eggs

I c. milk*

½ c. heavy cream*

3 tbsp. sugar

pinch of salt

I tsp. vanilla extract

ground or freshly grated nutmeg

1. Thinly butter bread. Cut each slice into four squares.

2. Arrange half of the bread in the bottom of a buttered, 1-quart casserole dish. Sprinkle raisins over bread and cover with remaining bread.

3. Beat eggs with milk, cream, sugar, salt, and vanilla. Pour egg mixture over the ingredients in the casserole. Let stand 30 minutes to allow milk mixture to soak into bread.

4. Preheat oven to 350°F. Sprinkle nutmeg over dessert. When oven is ready, bake 40 minutes, or until golden brown.

5. Serve custard warm, either by itself or with canned fruit.

Preparation time: 15 minutes
(plus 30 minutes standing time)
Baking time: 40 minutes
Serves 4 to 6

*Use skim milk and substitute evaporated skim milk for heavy cream to reduce the fat content of this dessert.

Holiday and Festival Food

Australian holiday gatherings and celebrations nearly always include a sampling of delicious, festive foods. To create these special meals, Australian cooks rely, in part, on traditions and old family recipes. But, like so much of Australian cuisine, the food eaten on special occasions reflects both the wide range of outside influences on the nation and the wealth of native ingredients. This rich variety helps to create new variations and new traditions over time.

The holiday recipes in this chapter are perfect to prepare for your friends or family on a special occasion. You can also prepare these dishes anytime, to turn an ordinary meal into a special event. Get a taste of celebrating the Australian way!

Served with roast vegetables, gravy, and mint sauce, roast leg of lamb makes any meal a festival in itself. (Recipes on page 60–63.)

Roast Leg of Lamb

Although diners at a shearing-time picnic usually have lamb chops roasted over the fire, you can get a taste of the outback with this delicious roast. Some families also enjoy this meal on Christmas, despite the heat!

I leg of lamb (5 to 8 lb.)

freshly ground or regular pepper to
    taste

*Follow these guidelines to determine
roasting time for the lamb: 2 hours for
a 5-lb. leg of lamb, 2 hours 20 minutes
for 6 lb., 2 hours 40 minutes for 7 lb.,
and 3 hours for 8 lb.

1. Check the supermarket label for the weight of the lamb to determine cooking time.* Be sure that the meat is at room temperature.

2. Preheat oven to 400°F.

3. Place lamb on a rack in a roasting pan. Rub pepper on the outer fat of the lamb.

4. Place roasting pan in oven and immediately turn the temperature down to 350°F. Roast for the determined cooking time. The lamb is done when a meat thermometer inserted into the center of the roast reads 150°F to 160°F.

5. Remove roast from the oven and place on a platter. Cover with aluminum foil and keep warm for 10 to 15 minutes. Serve lamb with roast vegetables, rich gravy, and mint sauce (see pages 61, 62, and 63).

Preparation time: 10 minutes
Cooking time: 2 to 3 hours
Serves 8 to 10

Roast Vegetables

These hearty vegetables round out a delicious meal of roast lamb. Served in larger portions without the roast lamb, they can also make an excellent vegetarian entrée.

6 potatoes

1 pumpkin or hard-shelled squash

8 carrots

8 parsnips

3 onions

drippings from roast lamb or
    vegetable oil

a sprinkling of your favorite dried
    herbs (good choices might be
    rosemary, thyme, or parsley)

salt and pepper to taste

1. Wash and peel vegetables. Cut potatoes into thirds, and cut pumpkin or squash into similar-sized pieces. Cut carrots and parsnips crosswise once. Remove onion skins and leave onions whole.*

2. Place potatoes and carrots in roasting pan with lamb about 1 hour and 15 minutes before roast will be done. By this time, there should be enough drippings from the meat to cover the bottom of the roasting pan. If not, add enough vegetable oil to cover the bottom of the pan thinly.

3. Fifteen minutes later, add pumpkin, parsnips, and onions. Sprinkle vegetables with herbs. Turn all vegetables two or three times while cooking so that they will be evenly cooked and golden all over.

4. When lamb is ready, vegetables should also be tender. Place vegetables around meat on serving platter. If necessary, add salt and pepper to taste. Cover and keep warm while making the gravy.

*To easily remove onion skins, cook onions in boiling water for about 2 minutes. Carefully remove the onions with a slotted spoon and let them cool. Dry with paper towels and slip the skins off.

Preparation time: 10 to 15 minutes
Cooking time: 1 hour and 15 minutes
Serves 6 to 8

Rich Gravy

Smooth gravy is the perfect accompaniment to a juicy roast.

4 tbsp. fat from roast, or vegetable oil

4 tbsp. all-purpose flour

2½ c. canned beef broth

¼ tsp. pepper

1. Pour the drippings (fat and juices) from the roasting pan into a cup and allow fat to rise to the top. Measure 4 tbsp. of fat into a saucepan. If there isn't enough, add vegetable oil to make 4 tbsp. Place pan over medium heat and sprinkle in flour. Stir continuously with a wire whisk or wooden spoon until the mixture is smooth and begins to brown.

2. Add beef broth and pepper to pan. Stirring continuously, bring to a boil. Continue to boil for 1 minute. The gravy is ready when it is smooth and thick.

Cooking time: 15 minutes
Makes 2½ cups

Mint Sauce

Australians love this sauce. The flavors of mint and vinegar provide a delicious contrast to the richness of the lamb.

½ c. firmly packed fresh mint leaves

2 tbsp. sugar

¼ tsp. salt

¼ tsp. freshly ground pepper

¼ c. boiling water

¼ c. cider or white vinegar

1. Wash mint thoroughly and dry sprigs between paper towels. Pluck the leaves from the stems and snip them into small pieces with kitchen shears.

2. In a small bowl, combine mint, sugar, salt, and pepper. Add boiling water and stir until sugar is dissolved. Add vinegar and mix well. Serve sauce from a little pitcher or gravy boat on the table.

Preparation time: 20 minutes
Makes ¾ cup

Damper

This classic bush tucker is the type that contestants in Australia Day bush cooking competitions might prepare. Bushmen baked their damper right in the campfire, but you can make it in your oven.

4 c. self-rising flour*

1 tsp. salt

1 tbsp. butter, softened

1 c. milk

½ c. water

1. Preheat oven to 425°F.

2. In a large bowl, stir together flour and salt. Using a pastry blender or two butter knives, cut in butter until dough has a coarse, crumbly texture.

3. Use your hands to make a hole in the center of the flour mixture. Pour milk and water into hole and stir until liquid is evenly distributed and dough holds together.

4. Turn the dough out onto a lightly floured countertop or other working surface and shape into a round loaf about 8 inches across. Place loaf onto a lightly greased cookie sheet and use a knife to cut a cross in the top of the dough.

5. Place dough in oven and bake at 425°F for 25 minutes. Lower oven temperature to 350°F and bake for 5 to 10 more minutes, or until loaf is golden brown and the bottom sounds hollow when tapped.

*Australian cooks—whether in the bush or the city—usually use self-rising flour to simplify their recipes. Look for self-rising flour at your supermarket or grocery store. If you have trouble finding it, simply add 1½ tsp. baking powder and ½ tsp. salt for every cup of all-purpose flour.

Preparation time: 25 to 30 minutes
Baking time: 30 to 40 minutes
Makes 1 loaf

Pavlova

This is the best-loved dessert in Australia. It is as light and delicate as the famous Russian ballerina Anna Pavlova, for whom it is named. It is best on the day it is made, and it is a favorite dessert on a summery Christmas Day.

4 egg whites*

pinch of salt

I c. sugar

½ tsp. vanilla extract

¾ tsp. white vinegar

I c. heavy whipping cream

kiwifruit, strawberries, bananas, passion fruit, or other fresh or well-drained

canned fruit of your choice

1. Cover a baking sheet with kitchen parchment paper or heavy-duty aluminum foil (dull side up). Using a bowl or plate, trace a 7-inch circle on the paper or foil. Preheat oven to 250°F.

2. Using an electric mixer, beat egg whites with salt until soft peaks form. Add ⅓ cup of sugar and beat until sugar is dissolved and mixture is very thick. Add remaining sugar one or two tbsp. at a time, beating well after each addition. When all sugar is dissolved and mixture is very stiff, add vanilla and vinegar. Beat well. The mixture, called a meringue, should be thick and glossy.

*To separate an egg, crack it cleanly on the edge of a nonplastic bowl. Holding the two halves of the eggshell over the bowl, gently pour the egg yolk back and forth between the two halves, letting the egg white drip into the bowl and being careful not to break the yolk. When most of the egg white has been separated, discard yolk.

3. Spoon meringue into the circle marked on the paper or foil. Using the back of a kitchen spoon, spread meringue out evenly within the circle. Build up the sides of the meringue to form a bowl shape.

4. Bake for 1½ hours, or until firm to the touch. Turn off the oven and allow the meringue to cool in the oven with the oven door ajar.

5. In a chilled bowl, whip heavy cream until stiff. Spread the whipped cream over the top of the pavlova. Wash and slice the fruit, using one kind of fruit or a combination of fruits. If using passion fruit, cut in half and scoop out the pulp. Arrange fruit attractively on top of whipped cream. Cut in wedges and serve immediately.

Preparation time: 10 to 15 minutes
Baking time: 1½ hours
Serves 8

Macadamia Nut Bread

Macadamia nuts have grown in Australia for centuries, and they are one of the ingredients prized by aboriginal cooks who attend celebrations such as the Bunya Festival. Unlike many of the native foods used by aborigines, which are not widely available outside Australia, macadamia nuts can be found at most grocery stores. Make this sweet bread to sample a delightful Australian flavor.

1 c. bran cereal, such as All-Bran

1 c. milk

½ c. macadamia nuts, chopped

½ c. dried apricots or candied cherries, chopped

1 c. sugar

1 c. self-rising flour

1. Preheat oven to 350°F.

2. Grease a 9 × 5-inch loaf pan.

3. In medium-sized mixing bowl, combine cereal and milk. Let stand 5 to 10 minutes while you chop nuts and dried or candied fruit.

4. Add sugar, flour, nuts, and fruit to cereal mixture. Mix well.

5. Spread bread batter evenly in prepared loaf pan. Bake 55 to 60 minutes, or until a toothpick inserted into the center of the loaf comes out clean. Carefully remove pan from oven and place on a wire rack to cool for 10 minutes.

6. Carefully remove loaf from pan. Allow loaf to cool on rack for about 2 hours, or until completely cool, before slicing. Wrap tightly and store at room temperature for up to four days, or refrigerate for up to ten days.

Preparation time: 15 minutes
Baking time: 55 to 60 minutes
Makes 1 loaf

Index

About the Authors

Elizabeth Germaine was born in Australia. She studied cooking at Invergowrie Homecraft Hostel in Melbourne and at Cordon Bleu Cooking School in London, England. She has been a recipe editor, has written several cookbooks and magazine articles, and has taught cooking classes. She and her husband live in Stillwater, Minnesota. They have two grown daughters and two grandchildren.

Ann L. Burckhardt was born and raised in Iowa. After earning her degree in home economics journalism at Iowa State University, she moved to Minnesota and became a Betty Crocker cookbook editor. From 1971 through 1995, she wrote for the *Minneapolis Star Tribune's* food section. She visited Australia in 1989 for a cooking conference there. She has written a textbook and four multicultural cookbooks. She lives in Burnsville, Minnesota.

Photo Acknowledgments

The photographs in this book are reproduced with the permission of: © Betty Crowell, pp. 2–3, 11; © Walter and Louiseann Pietrowicz/September 8th Stock, pp. 4 (left and right), 5 (left and right), 6, 18, 30, 35, 36, 40, 42, 45, 50, 52, 58, 65, 68; © John Penisten/Pacific Pictures, pp. 9, 13, 14, 17, 26; Robert L. & Diane Wolfe, p. 56.

Cover photos and spine: © Walter and Louiseann Pietrowicz/September 8th Stock, all.

The illustrations on pages 7, 19, 27, 31, 32, 33, 34, 37, 38, 39, 43, 44, 47, 49, 53, 54, 57, 59, 60, 61, 64, 66 are by Tim Seeley.
The map on page 8 is by Bill Hauser.